"A beautiful and well-writter [barcode] her side, Mary takes you on a li_____ ___ struggles and victories that encourage you to go deep with God until you experience your own victories.

Ron Hall, Author *Same Kind of Different as Me*, #1 *New York Times* Bestseller

"I liked Mary the first time I met her—in the bathroom at a conference. She flashed her bright smile and introduced herself, 'Hi, my name is Mary.' I smiled and shook her hand. I was impressed. I was even more impressed when she took the stage to tell her story: a story of courage, compassion and resilience.

Mary's memoir is a book for every woman who's ever struggled to balance career and home, productivity and procrastination, fear, faith, and self-acceptance. Mary's cancer diagnosis was the catalyst for her book, but the treasure was there long before. Mary's writing is funny, generous, and true. This is a book that stays with you."

Tina Sprinkle, Owner T School Retreats

Mary Meyer has been a successful entrepreneur, businesswoman, goal-setter, and cancer survivor, and now she has written *I Meant It for Good* to encourage others to find success and peace in all areas of their lives. I met Mary a number of years ago and encouraged her to follow my practice of setting goals in six key areas: Professional, Spiritual, Health, Relationships, Emotional, and Financial. Since then I've watched Mary dream, achieve, and soar to heights no one could have imagined. This book will show you how to do that too.

Dr. Tom Hill, Speaker, Author & Dreamer

"If you've ever met Mary, you know that she is genuine and sincere, just as her book portrays. This book is an inspiration for anyone who second guesses their own power. She shows how someone of a small stature exudes power through persistence and determination to heal. Truly remarkable."

Tina Asher, Owner Build U Up Consulting

Mary is a passionate, strong, and resilient warrior and champion for what's good in the world, and in this book, you will clearly get that feeling as you share her life's journey. At some point, we all have to deal with some kind of personal challenge; no one is immune. But it's how you choose to deal with those challenges that matters. When you read Mary's story, you will gain inspiration and strength, which you can draw upon when the need arises.

This book will not only become one of your favorite reads, but it will become one of those books that remains on your library shelves for quick reference. I highly recommend, *I Meant it for Good*, and I know you will soon realize that those very words and their intention shines through in the essence of her writing.

Alvin Brown, International speaker and author of
Journey to Personal Greatness: Mind, Body and Soul.
A Blueprint for Life Balance and Self-Mastery

I Meant It
for
Good

Mary Rechkemmer-Meyer

I Meant It for Good

A MEMOIR OF DREAMING, VISUALIZING, AND BECOMING MY AUTHENTIC SELF

Mary Rechkemmer-Meyer

Stonebrook Publishing
Saint Louis, Missouri

A STONEBROOK PUBLISHING BOOK
©2020 Mary Rechkemmer-Meyer

Library of Congress Control Number: 9781733995887
ISBN: 978-1-7339958-8-7

www.stonebrookpublishing.net
PRINTED IN THE UNITED STATES OF AMERICA
10 9 8 7 6 5 4 3 2 1

Contents

Preface

’ve wanted to write a book for a long time, but while I was raising a family and working, it never seemed to be the right time. Now that I've retired, I've finally run out of excuses! From this vantage point, I can look back at experiences that seemed like problems at the time and be grateful for the lessons I learned.

I waited until now to write this book because, in addition to being consumed with raising a family and work, in the past I listened to an inner voice that said, "Who are *you* to write a book?" My journey is probably not that different from yours. Because we're busy being what we think someone else wants us to be, we often need permission to live our own authentic lives. This experience can be especially true for women. My hope is that you will learn something from my life that will help you live your own life and follow your dreams.

My life has been far from perfect, but maybe that's why I needed to write this—to tell you that it's okay to be yourself. We've tried for too long to be "superwomen" who only show the side of ourselves that looks perfect. Or worse, we look at other people and think they're perfect because that's the only side they're willing to share. We are who we are, and we need to embrace ourselves fully—both the good and the not so good. We need to forgive ourselves for our failures and move forward. We need to allow ourselves to be human and to ask for help when we need it. We weren't meant to live in a vacuum.

I never knew how much growing up in a farming community with hard-working parents would affect my life. Nor did I know that what seemed to be hardships would become catalysts that moved me forward. While I got stuck many times, I've realized that you can either stay stuck or you can move forward. Is it easy? No. But whoever sold us on the idea that life would be easy? And what is easy anyway? Taking the easy way out isn't rewarding. Hard work, perseverance, and becoming your authentic self are all ways of being free and at peace. The struggle is rewarding and is what life is all about.

Where did my journey begin? My parents were farmers in North Dakota. My father owned a quarter section of land and farmed another quarter section with the help of my five older brothers. He had health problems and eventually had to sell the farm to pay the medical bills. Thinking that someday he'd buy another farm, he moved my mother and brothers to another farmstead, where I was born. I grew up on this farm and attended a one-room schoolhouse just down the road.

My parents were Mennonites, and I grew up in a conservative Christian environment. Now, don't get me wrong. My parents were very loving people. However, somewhere my interpretation of God became one of fear, not love. I remember coming home from Sunday school as a child with the little missionary stories they would hand out. Although I enjoyed reading them, in the back of my mind I was always afraid that if I listened to God, He would send me to the mission field in some faraway, scary place. Where did this fear come from? It was great work that the missionaries were doing, but I certainly didn't want to go so far away. I also remember hearing a lot about repentance and that we'd all sinned and were headed straight to hell if we didn't give our lives to God. What does this idea mean to a child? It's taken me years to truly understand my relationship with God and to see Him as a God of love, not fear.

Even though I grew up in a very conservative environment, I realize how privileged I was to grow up in a loving extended family that included aunts, uncles, and many cousins. Because we belonged to a small church, many of the church members were also like family.

Introduction

I was a shy child, and I sometimes felt like an only child because I was sandwiched between a brother who was six years older and a sister who was five years younger. How does a shy little girl tackle the world and learn to visualize her life? How does she learn to live the life she's dreamed of and grow to eventually visualize healing when faced with cancer?

Cancer has become an epidemic that we must be willing to examine. The way we're treating cancer isn't working. Are we willing to step out of our "boxes" and look at other ways of preventing and treating cancer, or are we going to stick our heads in the sand, unwilling to look at the problem? My hope is that you will be open-minded and know that you have options before you're in a crisis. We live in a very divided, negative world, and I don't mean to say that my way is the only way.

There are many ways to heal and prevent cancer. This book is about believing in yourself. I want you to believe that if you ever hear the horrific words, "You have cancer," you'll know where to turn, what to do, and whom to see—but most importantly, you'll be able to visualize healing and believe that you can be healed. This book is ultimately about my journey through life, how I grew up, the challenges I faced, and how I learned to set and achieve goals and to believe in myself and in God. The exercises in each chapter are about setting goals in all areas of your life, a practice that has made me the woman I am today.

This book is ultimately about my journey through life, how I grew up, the challenges I faced, and how I learned to set and achieve goals and to believe in myself and in God.

We all have adversities and hardships that can either challenge us to succeed or break us. We're all on a different journey. I've seen people whose lives were much harder than mine who've inspired me to be a better person. I've also seen those who buckled under the pressure. Isn't it wonderful that we get to pick which road to take?

The Road Not Taken
by Robert Frost

Two roads diverged in a yellow wood,
And sorry I could not travel both
And be one traveler, long I stood
And looked down one as far as I could
To where it bent in the undergrowth;

Then took the other, as just as fair,
And having perhaps the better claim,
Because it was grassy and wanted wear;
Though as for that the passing there
Had worn them really about the same,

And both that morning equally lay
In leaves no step had trodden black.
Oh, I kept the first for another day!
Yet knowing how way leads on to way,
I doubted if I should ever come back.

I shall be telling this with a sigh
Somewhere ages and ages hence:
Two roads diverged in a wood, and I—
I took the one less traveled by,
And that has made all the difference.

CHAPTER 1

The Beginning

"As you read my stories of long ago, I hope you will remember that things truly worthwhile and that will give you happiness are the same now as they were then. It is not the things you have that make you happy. It is love and kindness and helping each other and just plain being good."

~ Laura Ingalls Wilder

I stood in my room, sobbing. I felt like someone had just punched me in the gut. I didn't have words for what had just happened. My husband, Jan, heard my sobs and came into the room. He asked me what was wrong, but the sound of his voice was surreal. I wasn't sure if I was dreaming or if this was actually happening. He asked me what was wrong. Had I been on the phone? I nodded my head, because no words would form in my mouth. I was finally able to speak but had a hard time telling him what had happened. He asked me who I'd been talking to. I told him it was the doctor.

"You mean the doctor you saw yesterday who got upset with you and asked if you wanted her to examine you or if you just wanted to leave?"

I nodded. Yes, that was the one.

"She said that my blood work came back and I have leukemia. She's already talked to a hematologist, but because it's so advanced, they don't want me to wait to see a specialist. Instead, the hematologist will call the emergency room doctor and tell that doctor how to do a bone-marrow biopsy. She said to get to the emergency room right away because the cancer is so advanced, they need to start treatment immediately."

Jan said, "Wait! She told you all this over the phone?"

I nodded.

When I was a child, I'd play in a grove of trees that had been cleared to make a playhouse. I lined up my dolls and talked to them. I was the teacher and they were the students. It was here that I'd make the proverbial mud pies with my cousins. Much later, I realized that this playhouse was where I began to imagine getting married one day, having children, and being a housewife. That future I saw was modeled by the women in my life, and I don't believe I ever thought about doing anything different.

We lived in an old farmhouse on the North Dakota prairie. Although we were poor at the time, I didn't know it because we raised cattle and hogs and grew our own vegetables. We always had an abundance of food. We shared big family meals, and if we weren't entertaining family and friends, we were often visiting them at their homes. I witnessed the hard work it took to run a farm and raise a family, and that was my normal. My father had health problems and, as they worsened, it became harder and harder for him to farm.

The oldest of eleven children, my mother had quit school after eighth grade to help care for her siblings. Hard work was nothing new to her. She had a huge vegetable garden, and each summer she would can food for the coming winter. She not only cooked the traditional big meals for us and the farmhands, but also made clothes for my sister, Janet, and me.

We didn't have electricity, so we'd read by the light of gas lamps in the evening. I remember that one Christmas I got a wind-up record player. I had some vinyl records that came with the player, but what I remember playing most often were the records I cut out of cereal boxes. Recently, Janet and I had a conversation about that old record player.

"I still remember getting that for Christmas," she said.

"That wasn't yours," I said. "I got it for Christmas."

"Are you kidding me?" she answered. "I thought that was mine and everything else was a hand-me-down! Now you're telling me that wasn't even mine." Oops!

I was educated in a one-room schoolhouse. It was hard to think of myself as being in any particular grade because I could see and hear every lesson and assignment from grades one through eight. I couldn't wait to get my book about Dick and Jane and to be able to read it by myself. I loved to sit at my desk and look through my new books. I loved

I was educated in a one-room schoolhouse. It was hard to think of myself as being in any particular grade because I could see and hear every lesson and assignment from grades one through eight.

the feel and the smell of them—not only the books assigned for class, but my library books as well. We had a library in the corner of the room where you could check out your own books just by writing your name on a card and filing it in a box. Oh, how grown up I felt! I'd never been to a library before.

And the playground equipment—whatever happened to teeter-totters and merry-go-rounds? I wonder how many times I came crashing to the ground when someone larger than I controlled the teeter-totter. And how many times did I get sick and dizzy on the merry-go-round but still insist on more? I didn't know that the teeter-totter would become a symbol of the ups and downs in my life, and the merry-go-round—well, haven't we all been on the merry-go-round of life?

Walking up the steps to the little schoolhouse after recess, I could often smell the aroma of soup being cooked over the one-burner camp stove—soup that would accompany the sandwich I'd brought from home in my Dale Evans and Roy Rogers lunch box.

It seems strange that I wore a dress every day as a child, but I did. I didn't own anything but dresses. One Christmas, I was in a school program and my mother bought me a new blouse and a felt circle skirt that I loved to twirl around in with my new black suede shoes. I was so proud of this outfit, and I'm sure it was the first clothing I owned that was not homemade.

When I was in fourth grade, my father gave up farming and moved us to town. What a culture shock for this little farmer's daughter! We moved in the middle of the school year, which meant I went from that little one-room schoolhouse to a fourth-grade class of thirty children. I became sick almost every day, but most days I made it to the bathroom before my stomach revolted and I lost my breakfast or lunch.

I'd nearly made it through fourth grade and was just getting acclimated to life in town when we took our standardized tests at the end of the year. When the results came back, the school administrators suggested to my parents that I skip fifth grade. I'm sure attending that one-room schoolhouse and hearing the lessons for every grade had something to do with this recommendation.

I jumped ahead to sixth grade, and now I had to start making friends all over again. I was a small child, and some of my older classmates looked more like adults than children. I became close friends with five other girls. This little country girl learned a lot from the city girls. Amazingly, the six of us are still in touch.

In North Dakota at that time, you could get your driver's license at age fourteen, which meant I was thirteen when my friends got their licenses. We had fun cruising around looking for boys. I don't know why anyone thought this was a good idea, as I grew up way too fast. Well, at least I thought I was grown up.

EXERCISE: CHAPTER 1

Have you neglected your inner child? Is she crying for attention? Much has been written about the inner child. We've often been told that we just need to grow up, but to grow up healthy, we need to remember who we were as children and listen to what those children are saying to us.

- What are your earliest memories of childhood? Are they good memories?
- Look at pictures from your childhood. What did you like to do as a child? Do you still allow time for play? Many of us have become goal-oriented and forgotten how to play.
- Can you go back and recapture the innocence of your childhood and be at peace? How can you do that?

CHAPTER 2

Down the Chute
They Come—
Oh, Baby!

*"It is no small thing, when they, who are so
fresh from God, love us."*

~ Charles Dickens

C oming of age in high school is always a struggle, but for
me this particular time also brought a struggle regarding
religion. At the time, I didn't think too deeply about it, but
I knew I didn't want to follow the rules and regulations that went
along with my conservative upbringing. I wanted to have a good time.

I graduated from high school in 1965 and had the whole world ahead of me. The next summer, I worked and prepared to start cosmetology school in the fall. While I'd soon learn that cosmetology wasn't what I wanted to do with my life, I'd learned that if you start something, you must finish it. Eventually, I quit cosmetology school—and I felt like a failure.

Shortly afterward, I moved to Illinois and started working for the local telephone company. I had no idea what I really wanted to do, but I was pretty sure I'd get married and have children. And sure enough, that's exactly what happened.

I was married in 1967, and the babies soon followed. Down the chute came the first one—a little boy we named Shawn. We marveled over this precious, tiny life. Could it get any better than this? Two years later, we had a little girl who stole our hearts. We named her Jodi. We were like children raising children. We watched our children grow and marveled at how they changed from day to day. Eight years later, we had another son, Brian. He couldn't have been loved more—not only by his parents but by his siblings as well. Two years later, baby Melissa arrived with a full head of black hair and, once again, she stole our hearts. We were truly blessed.

I made a conscious decision to stay home and raise my children. I couldn't imagine entrusting them to anyone else. Anyone who knows me knows that I'm somewhat of a control freak, and I wanted to instill my own values in my children. Did I always do a good job? No. But I gave it my best shot. I knew I didn't have all the answers, but I also knew my children were my responsibility. I think it was just such a different time back then. I'm not sure if I had it to do over again that I'd stay home for so many years. Maybe I would have worked part-time. I've always said the hardest thing I've ever done is stay at home and raise four children. However, I feel blessed to have been able to stay home with my children when they were growing up.

Life was busy with four children, and some days it seemed there would never be time for myself. I realize that I took on the life that was modeled by my parents. I had a large garden, from which I preserved a lot of the family's food. I learned to sew clothes for myself and my daughters. I worked hard and became a perfectionist because I thought that was a good thing. I believed that if I stayed home to raise the children, then my job was to do everything associated with the home: cooking, cleaning, sewing, canning, freezing—you name it. Someone always needed something when the children were young. As they got a little older, I became involved in my community and church, as well as their school activities. I'm so happy I had this time with them, even though it wasn't always easy. It's hard to find that balance of keeping busy and giving back without giving too much of yourself and feeling depleted.

I'd be remiss if I didn't tell you that when my youngest two were still small, I went through a terrible depression. At the time, I thought it would be something I'd never forget. Yet somehow, I've forgotten a lot of it. Quite frankly, I think this experience may have been the beginning of my search to discover who I am.

But the depression scared me. I felt like I was in a manhole, and just as I'd get my fingers to the edge of the hole to pull myself up, I'd slide back down. I went to counseling for the first time in my life and would learn that it takes a strong person to go to counseling to find out who they really are. I learned that you need to live your true life, not the life someone thinks you should live,

I grew up in a conservative environment where I learned only one way to live. Later, I learned that this way didn't reflect who I really was.

and not the life you think you should live based on someone else's idea of what's right for you.

I grew up in a conservative environment where I learned only one way to live. Later, I learned that this way didn't reflect who I really was. I needed to find out what I truly believed and to make it mine. After high school, I'd stopped going to church. When I had children, however, I knew I wanted to raise them in a church and instill in them the spiritual principles with which I'd been raised. When I was questioning my faith, it was a blessing that I didn't "throw the baby out with the bathwater."

I've come to realize how important my faith is to me. I once listened to a CD about the two "containers of life." The first container is the law. If we don't learn the law or teach our children the law—whether it's biblical law or governmental law—they'll have no ethical basis and will easily get into trouble. However, this speaker went on to say that once we've learned the law, we're in the second container and can then live by grace. Why is it so hard for us to extend grace to others if God has extended grace to us? Why are we so quick to judge others and not let them be free to live their lives? We need to learn how to be free, to live by grace, and then extend that grace to others.

And let's face it, anyone who's been home with small children knows how demanding it is. You're the one taking care of their every need, but who takes care of you? I wish I'd taken more time to nurture myself and to ask for help when I needed it, instead of thinking I had to carry the whole burden by myself.

Yet, I learned life skills as a mother that would be useful in later years. I was once asked if I'd ever sold anything. I said, "Are you kidding? I sell my kids on my ideas every day." Of course, that was true only until they got older and knew everything!

How truly blessed I've been to be a mother to these four children and to now be a grandmother to their children. I'm so proud to be called Mother and Grandmother.

EXERCISE: CHAPTER 2

- What were your struggles growing up?
- Did you face anything that seems to be contrary to what you believe today?
- Did you do things just because you felt it was required of you?
- Do you think everyone has to believe exactly like you?

CHAPTER 3

Coming of Age for the Second Time

"If you don't design your own life plan, chances are you'll fall into someone else's plan. And guess what they have planned for you? Not much."

~ Jim Rohn

I n 1989, I went back to work after being a housewife for twenty-two years. I remember waking up one morning, sitting up in bed, and thinking, "I'm going back to work." Now I ask you: Where did that idea come from? I believe it was from God—the source of the still, small voice inside me. The thought simply wouldn't go away.

I went to a friend's house and told her what I was thinking, and she said, "Let's write up a resume." So that's exactly what we did. Remember, I hadn't worked in twenty-two years and had never gone to college, so it was a challenge to come up with something I could put on a resume. But that didn't stop us. We wrote a resume and sent it out. Then I sat back and waited to hear what would happen. I waited and waited and waited.

I obviously needed to take another approach, so I went to the local junior college and took a refresher typing class and an accounting class. I was just finishing these classes when a friend called who'd heard I was looking for a job. He worked at a local trucking company and said they were looking for someone to handle their accounts payable. I told him I was interested, but my children would soon be out of school for the summer, and I probably couldn't start working until the fall when they went back to school. He insisted that I come in and talk to them. He was sure I could start out with a few hours a week and increase it to more hours in the fall. And that's exactly what I did.

What an exciting time it was for me, going back to work! Yet, it didn't come without challenges. Because I'd been home for so many years raising children, I felt guilty when I wasn't there all the time. It was hard not to lose my identity when I was raising children. I don't know how many times I was called Shawn's mother, or Jodi's mother, or Brian's mother, or Melissa's mother. After a while I thought of myself in those terms.

Not long after, my husband and I flew to Florida for our twenty-fifth anniversary and spent a week on Sanibel Island. It was the first time I'd ever flown on an airplane. I felt like my whole life was opening before me. I had a new freedom from working part time, two of my children were raised and married, and I saw glimpses of what I could do after all the children were out of the house.

But within a couple of months, things unraveled in our marriage. My husband decided he no longer wanted to be married. Of course we had our share of problems, but divorce was not on my radar. I was devastated and felt like someone had put a fist through my gut. How would I survive? I'd stayed home to raise the children and had only been working part time for three years. I'd married young and hadn't gone to college. I never thought this could happen to me. To other people, yes—but not to me. I certainly wasn't making enough money to support myself, and my health insurance came through my husband's work. I didn't even have a credit card in my own name.

I was angry. I thought my world had ended. By the grace of God, I pulled myself together enough to believe that I could support myself. I went to counseling; I knew that I needed to put my life back together. Not to restore it to the way it was before, but to believe that God had another plan.

> I'd stayed home to raise the children and had only been working part time for three years. I'd married young and hadn't gone to college. I never thought this could happen to me ... I didn't even have a credit card in my own name.

A friend of mine gave me the following verse: "For I know the plans I have for you," declares the Lord, "plans to prosper you and not to harm you, plans to give you hope and a future" (Jeremiah 29:11 NIV). I clung to this verse. And I started to see synchronicities showing up in my life, or as some people would call them, God Winks. Everywhere I went, I'd see this verse, yet before then I'd never heard it.

I went to a divorce seminar, read more books, and met new friends. These friends became like family to me. For the first time in my life, I was able to share myself at a gut level. Had my prior life been only an act? I looked back all the way to high school and realized that my friends and I had never shared anything important to us. Was this the way women lived then? Did we think every other woman was June Cleaver, and since we couldn't measure up, we didn't share? I think it actually goes deeper than that. Growing up in the 1950s and, '60s, it wasn't the norm to talk about your feelings. People didn't write self-help books back then, and we certainly didn't talk about personal problems.

My anger motivated me to keep moving. The company I worked for gave me full-time hours with benefits, a change for which I'll always be grateful. I started taking night classes again. I realized that I could support myself, but that I'd need to start looking for a new career in a larger organization.

My friends started telling me that I ought to look at State Farm in Bloomington, Illinois because of the benefits and opportunities the company offered. I couldn't imagine driving forty miles to and from Bloomington every day. What would I do in the winter when the roads were bad? I'd lived a pretty sheltered life, and if I was going to stretch and grow, I'd have to get out of my "box."

I didn't even consider the opportunity until the sixth person said to me, "You need to be at State Farm. My kids work there, and I'll have them send you an application." When I received the application, I filled it out and was eventually hired full time in the accounting department at the Illinois regional office in Bloomington. I continued to go to night school.

My life was pretty much a blur. I was up before 5:00 a.m. every morning, then I'd drive forty miles to Bloomington, work until 4:00 p.m., then drive forty miles back home. My evenings consisted of going to class or staying home and studying for the next class. Two nights a week, I went to class from 6:00 p.m. to 10:00 p.m., and I earned a total of eight credit hours per semester.

In addition, they offered weekend classes on Friday nights and all day on Saturdays and Sundays, and students could take three weekend classes per semester to earn an additional four hours. I took twelve hours per semester and worked full time.

I almost had a panic attack when I learned I'd have to write a ten-page term paper. How would I ever write ten pages? But with each additional term paper, the writing became progressively easier.

I had to dig deep to spur myself on, to believe that I could do this. I had my vision, and I couldn't let it out of my sight—even on the days when I didn't believe it. People asked me how I did it all—working and going to school. Although it was difficult, it was something I needed to do. As hard as night school was, I learned a lot about myself and what I wanted to do during this time. I learned to believe in myself.

I had to dig deep to spur myself on, to believe that I could do this. I had my vision, and I couldn't let it out of my sight—even on the days when I didn't believe it.

Two of my children still lived at home, but my other two lived in the suburbs of Detroit and Indianapolis. The thought of driving to either of these places was frightening, and I initially felt I couldn't do it. But the more I thought about it, I knew I was only hurting myself by not going to visit them. If other people could drive that far, then so could I. How liberating it was to learn to do these things, and what confidence it gave me each time I tried something new!

This wasn't an easy time of life. I'd never want to go through it again, nor would I wish it on my worst enemy, but I wouldn't give up the growth I gained for anything. The biggest lesson I learned through my divorce was the power of forgiveness. Forgiveness is not for the other person. Forgiveness is a release for yourself. Forgiveness is getting to a place inside yourself where you can release the anger and be at peace, regardless of what the other party says, thinks, or does. Ultimately, forgiveness is between you and God—no one else.

I learned to forgive before I felt like doing it. I asked God to help me forgive day after day, until one day I woke up and realized that I really meant it. And I was released. When I took one step forward, God dragged me forward two more steps. I'd heard this process likened to a verse from Psalms: "Your word is a lamp to my feet and a light to my path" (Psalm 119:105 NKJV). The person who shared this with me went on to explain that before electricity and gas lamps, people strapped a candle to their feet, so they could see the path in front of them, thus illuminating the path only as they took each step forward.

EXERCISE: CHAPTER 3

- Describe a time when you were doing something because you felt like you *should* do it, not because you *wanted* to do it?
- Who can you talk to about things that are happening in your life, or do you keep everything bottled up inside?
- What adventures would you like to go on but are afraid to do so? How will you overcome that fear?
- Who do you need to forgive?

CHAPTER 4

State Farm Agency

"Failure will never overtake me if my determination to succeed is strong enough."

~ Og Mandino

I continued to take night classes and eventually completed the requirements to get my bachelor's degree, something I couldn't have visualized when I first started taking classes. But step by step, class by class, I achieved it.

Around the time of my graduation, State Farm offered a program for employees to learn about becoming an agent. I knew that whether I became a State Farm agent or used my degree to work in management, either was a great career path. After much consideration, I decided to find out if being a State Farm agent would be a good match for me.

It was a real stretch for me. I was much older than the others, but taking management classes at the college level had taught me to believe I could make a life for myself. I read Stephen Covey's *The 7 Habits of Highly Effective People* and thought about how to begin with the end in mind. I visualized myself as an agent, sitting behind a desk in a State Farm office. I also volunteered to work alongside two agents—just to see if this career was something I wanted and could do. I found out that I loved sales, which actually boiled down to the activities I'd been doing for years: telling stories and helping people.

> *It was a real stretch for me ... but taking management classes at the college level had taught me to believe I could make a life for myself.*

Now came the hard part: interviewing with three different groups of agents and the State Farm leadership. I would have to sit at the end of the long conference table in the executive office and answer all their questions. The day before my interview, I walked to that office and sat in the chair at the end of the table and visualized myself answering their questions. It must have worked, because after my interview I was approved to be a State Farm agent.

The company asked their agents to pick an area where they wanted to live. The expectation was that you'd take the next opportunity that was available in that area. I was offered an agency in Shelbyville, Illinois, so I sold my house in Morton and moved to this new town of 5,000 people. I didn't know a soul. My children were all out of the house by then, and this move was the beginning of my new life.

Shelbyville was a beautiful little town. I met with a real estate agent, who later became a great friend, and told her I was looking for a condo. I'd just sold my house and didn't want to take care of another one by myself. It soon became apparent that I wouldn't find a condo, so we started searching for houses, and I fell in love with one in a country subdivision on an acre and a half—a far cry from that condo I thought I'd wanted. The house backed up to wooded property owned by the Army Corps of Engineers along Lake Shelbyville. What a healing retreat it became, not only for me, but for many other people in my life. It was a peaceful place to call home, and the neighbors were all amazing.

It took a huge step of faith to purchase a house by myself. I'd never bought anything as expensive as this on my own, and I was working in sales with a commission-based income. If that wasn't enough pressure, I also bought the building where my office was located—an agonizing decision that turned out to be one of the best I ever made.

> With much excitement, I opened my own State Farm office ... For a long time, I'd visualized myself sitting behind this desk.

With much excitement, I opened my own State Farm office and was energized by this opportunity to start my own business. For a long time, I'd visualized myself sitting behind this desk. Because I was a new agent, if I wanted to be offered a contract at the end of my first year, I had to sell a certain amount of insurance in each line that State Farm represented: auto, fire, life, and health. The motivation and drive I'd mustered while working full time and going to school at night served me well. I attacked my new challenges in much the same way, setting appointments and meeting with people during the day and into the evening. I not only earned my contract by the end of the year, I also earned reward trips that allowed me to travel to wonderful places.

I'd been a stranger when I first moved to Shelbyville, but the people embraced me with open arms. They showed up in my office to help me along the journey, and they took me in and made me feel like their town was my town. I was honored to be a part of the community, and I soon joined the Kiwanis and the American Business Women's Association. I also had the privilege of serving on the Board of the Chamber of Commerce.

The book *Synchronicity: The Inner Path of Leadership* by Joseph Jaworski really spoke to me during this time. It's a story of people and circumstances that show up in your life when you're following your heart and what you believe to be the right path. I love the last sentence in the book: "Invoked or not invoked, God is present." In Shelbyville, I saw the synchronicities, and I knew God was at work.

This life of hard work, fun travel, and community involvement was enjoyable for a while because I was single and my children were grown. But I felt that something was missing. I was alone in a small town. Yes, I had a lot of friends, but I always came home by myself, to myself. I began to ask myself, "What do I really believe?" and, "What's my purpose?" and, "What do I really want to do?"

So I searched inside to discover who I was. Along the journey, I read books that were "outside the box" for me. For example, I read books by Emmet Fox. Although I didn't agree with everything he said, his books led me to see my faith walk in a different light. I found out that some of the Bible verses I'd learned could be interpreted in different ways, and I felt God speaking to me when I thought them in another way.

We each have our own journey, and to believe that we can read a book or listen to a speaker and agree one hundred percent with him or her without challenging any of our own beliefs is a discredit to us. We need to stretch and grow. We need to listen to the still, small voice inside. God couldn't have spoken to me if I thought it had to be through a certain book or a certain person. I would have been limiting God. The truth is that God can speak through any book and any author.

I also read *The Road Less Traveled: A New Psychology of Love, Values, and Spiritual Growth* by M. Scott Peck. Again, did I agree with everything? No. But the book did resonate with me, and I learned a lot about relationships, the difference between dependency and love, and how to become your own true self. I spent a lot of time in my car, and I listened to many CDs from authors such as Jack Canfield, Mark Victor Hansen, and Jim Rohn. I was searching for what *I* really believed, not what someone had told me I *should* believe. And the more I read, the more I searched.

During this time I attended a "Walk to Emmaus" retreat—a three-day experience to strengthen and renew my faith. It was a healing time for me. I listened to the speakers talk about their journeys through life, and I became immersed in the program. There was an atmosphere of unconditional love, and I gained so much from this experience that I volunteered at several retreats after that and even went on to share my own story as a retreat speaker. Any time we share and give back to others, we learn a lot about ourselves.

EXERCISE: CHAPTER 4

- What do you really believe?
- What's your purpose?
- What do you really want to do with your life?
- Do you read books that will make you think outside of your "box"?
- Do you have to agree with everything you read? What happens if you don't?

CHAPTER 5

Dr. Tom Hill

"The way to get started is to quit talking and start doing."

~ Walt Disney

I attended a State Farm workshop where one of the speakers was Dr. Tom Hill. He spoke about having balance in all areas of life. As I sat there, I cried because I knew how to make my business work, but I was way out of balance in every other area of life.

Dr. Hill talked about these six areas of life:

- Spiritual
- Health and Wellness
- Relationships
- Emotional
- Professional and Intellectual
- Financial

Spiritual: Being at Peace with God

As I listened to Dr. Hill, I realized I'd only experienced fleeting moments of peace, which were followed by panic about things that needed to be done and relationships that weren't working the way I wanted.

Health and Wellness

There was really nothing about this topic that I didn't already know. The problem was that I hadn't implemented what I knew. I was too busy working day and night and had no peace about what I needed to do.

Relationships

As I listened to Dr. Hill, I thought to myself, "I'm single. I don't have a significant other. How can I carve out more time for someone else? What about my other relationships? Are they where I want them to be?"

Emotional

I was reading the books I needed to read for work, but were they getting me to the healthy and balanced life that I said I wanted? I had a lot of work to do here.

Financial

I was doing quite well financially, but there was a whole new world out there, and I felt like I'd limited myself.

Wow! Where to begin? How could I find that elusive balance in life? I started by reading the dozens of books on Dr. Hill's suggested reading list. I devoured each one and wondered why I didn't already know these things. To find balance, I first had to realize how out of balance I was.

I later attended another one of Dr. Hill's workshops, where he agreed to coach me. I learned that discipline is the key in every area of life. I'm a dreamer, so it's easier for me than it is for others to dream about what I want. But that's precisely when the little voice inside me—the voice that wasn't God—said, "Who are you to think you can do this?" Or, "What will people think?" It was easy for me to get bogged down right there. But whenever I did something important, I always felt a little scared and then moved ahead with intention and purpose. Fake it till you make it. Easy? No, but if it was, we'd all be living our dreams.

> *I learned to set goals and follow them through to the desired result.*

I learned to set goals and follow them through to the desired result. In my business, for example, I set goals to sell enough insurance to earn trips to London and Paris, as well as an Alaskan cruise.

My spiritual goal was to be at peace with God, so I started reading books that would help me achieve that. I also learned to be still before God and to meditate. I took classes to become a Stephen Minister, so I could give back to others.

Health and wellness were important to me because if I didn't have my health, I wouldn't have much. I started working on my diet and exercise. Slowly but surely, I set goals that I could achieve.

But the area of relationships eluded me. I had a lot of good friends, but it was hard to find that special someone with whom I wanted to spend the rest of my life.

As one of Dr. Hills's coaching students, twice a year I attended the Eagle Summit, where he brought in remarkable motivational speakers from every walk of life. I learned so much from this extremely positive group of people about setting goals and finding balance in my life, being an entrepreneur, and practicing meditation. I learned principles that would help me navigate through rough patches in the years ahead. I learned to set and achieve goals in the present and to map out long-term goals to define a vision about what my perfect world would look like six years in the future. In that vision, I saw myself sitting on my patio in a warm climate, holding a cup of coffee in the morning and a glass of wine in the evening while I watched the sun go down. This vision was crystal clear to me long before I would buy a house in Arizona.

EXERCISE: CHAPTER FIVE

Most of us are pretty good at setting goals. But are your goals taking you where you want to go? Have you set goals in *all* areas of your life? After you achieve one goal, do you have other goals in place so that you always have something to work toward? What about retirement goals? Will you be able to retire when you want to? Will you get to do the things in retirement you've always wanted to do? Will you continue setting goals in retirement?

Here's how to get started:

1. First, look at each area of your life based on the six components I learned from Dr. Tom Hill that make up a balanced life:
   a. Spiritual
   b. Health and Wellness
   c. Relationships
   d. Emotional
   e. Professional and Intellectual
   f. Financial

   Determine what's important to you.

2. Rank each area. On a scale of one to ten, with ten being the highest, where do you rate yourself? Are you out of balance in any of these areas? Think of each one of these areas as a spoke in a bicycle tire. If one spoke is broken or not working at capacity, the wheel will be out of balance.

3. Now list each of these areas in order of importance. They're listed above in order of their importance to me, but you should reorder them to reflect your own values.

4. What do you believe about each of these areas? What does each one mean to you? What book can you read or who do you know who can help you understand and move closer to your dream in each of these areas? The more clarity you get, the more focused you will be.

CHAPTER 6

Dating at Fifty

"Synchronicity is an ever-present reality for those who have eyes to see."

~ Carl Jung

While I didn't do the best job of dating as a teenager, let me say that at age fifty dating was a completely different ballgame. The whole thing was awkward, although sometimes it was exciting. People would set me up with a friend of theirs that they just *knew* was the right person for me. What were they thinking? Did they know me at all? Then there were the people I met and tried to date. Another strikeout—what were we thinking? And then I tried dating services. Did these services really think this person was a match for me?

A friend once told me that what I was experiencing was the law of large numbers; you had to meet a lot of men to find the right one. So I started meeting men for lunch dates because it would be easier to leave if the conversation didn't go anywhere. But how many lunches do you have to have before Mr. Right comes along?

I knew I needed something more. I heard about a Christian dating service in Saint Louis, run by a woman named Jeannie who came highly recommended. She also had an office in Jerseyville, Illinois, which was near Shelbyville, where I lived. I was tired of meeting men who didn't have a spiritual foundation, so I tried her service.

> *So, I started meeting men for lunch dates because it would be easier to leave if the conversation didn't go anywhere.*

Jeannie was quite a matchmaker. Her business was an old-fashioned matchmaking business. She wasn't online, but she had books filled with client photographs and bios. She flipped through the books and pointed to someone's photo and said, "You would really like him." I agreed to meet several of the men, and she sent each of them my bio. If they wanted to contact me, they would do so. When she met new clients who wanted to meet me, she'd forward their bios to me, and it was up to me to contact them if I was interested. It was a long process, and sometimes I thought, *What was Jeannie thinking?* after I met the man.

About six months later, I received a new photo and bio and thought to myself, "He's really cute." So, I called him. And guess what? He didn't return my call. But I was in sales, so I called him back. Long story short, two years later Jan and I were married. To this day, Jan claims that he was on vacation when I called the first time, and that's why he didn't call me back. I'd say it was another one of those synchronicities that can't be explained, other than that God was at work.

EXERCISE: CHAPTER 6

I couldn't work on all six areas of balance in my life at the same time, so I picked two or three to work on at one time. The area of relationships was the one that had continued to elude me. Take a look at the questions below to identify the areas you want to focus on first:

- In what area do you want to start setting goals?
- Which areas do you work on more than the others?
- Which areas elude you?
- In what area do you need help, and who will you ask to help you?

CHAPTER 7

Married Again

"You can't go back and change the beginning, but you can start where you are and change the ending."

~ C. S. Lewis

After dating for two years, Jan and I decided to marry. How hard could it be to get my four children and Jan's three children and all our grandchildren to the wedding? I wanted to get married in June, but we couldn't find a date that worked for everyone. I didn't want to get married after that because my youngest daughter, Melissa, was getting married in September, and I wanted to focus on her wedding.

Melissa suggested we get married on July first because there'd be a long weekend over the fourth of July. But I'd earned a trip to London for selling life insurance, and we were leaving on July fourth. I didn't want to go on my honeymoon "with all the State Farm people." But Jan and I finally decided to marry on July first, then honeymoon in London. After all, how many people get to do that?

We got married in my backyard in Shelbyville. We had planned a small wedding, inviting only family and a few friends. But in the end, we had eighty guests. We hired a string trio that played before the wedding, and I walked out to meet Jan to the strains of Pachelbel's "Canon in D". What could be more romantic?

In London, we stayed across from Hyde Park and shopped at Harrods Department Store, where we picked up a loaf of bread, some cheese, and a bottle of wine so we could picnic in the park as we watched the Queen's Cavalry ride by. We went to several spectacular plays in intimate, stunningly ornate theaters. At Buckingham Palace, we watched the changing of the guard. We visited Windsor Castle and Eaton and rode the London Eye. We took the Chunnel from London to Paris, where we went up to the second level of the Eiffel Tower and back down to the street for lunch. We also toured the Seine River and, from there, we saw beautiful cathedrals, bridges, and other wonderful sights. We entered the Louvre Museum and saw the *Mona Lisa*. We were certainly blessed.

Eventually, we came home to the real world. To say we had our share of problems doesn't adequately describe our life. Although we were clearly adults, we both had a lot of growing up to do. There were times, quite frankly, when we each looked at one another and thought,

> *To say we had our share of problems doesn't adequately describe our life. Although we were clearly adults, we both had a lot of growing up to do.*

What are you thinking? I've been doing this for fifty years, and I certainly wouldn't do it any other way. One of the best books that I've read on relationships, Matt Townsend's *Starved Stuff: Feeding the 7 Basic Needs of Healthy Relationships*, really helped me at the time.

And yet, we were so happy to have found each other and to travel this life together. Is marriage easy? No. Obviously, I didn't get it right the first time around. However, Jan and I have something special.

Jan was a farm manager and owned a house in Champaign, Illinois, and I was a State Farm Agent and still had my house in Shelbyville. We commuted every day from one house or the other. The one-and-a-half-hour commute was too much for both of us, and we couldn't seem to figure out how to make it work. After much agonizing, I decided to walk away from my career at State Farm—a decision that led me to question whether I'd done the right thing. But it's what needed to be done to make our marriage work.

Out of that adversity came many blessings. After I sold my home and the building that I'd purchased, I was able to buy a retirement home in Arizona with the proceeds—the one where I'd visualized sitting with my coffee or wine and enjoying the sunset. We rented out the Arizona house for eight years until we could start using it as our winter home.

Dr. Hill encouraged me to take a three-day silent retreat. I was to have no outside contact with anyone during this time. The first challenge was to quiet my mind from the things it told me that needed to be done. Initially, it was hard. How can you be silent for three whole days? But as the time progressed, I felt more peaceful and purposeful. I've been on several of these three-day retreats and have learned to be quiet and listen to the still, small voice.

As Jan and I struggled to find common ground in our marriage, I heard about a week-long silent retreat at a monastery in Ohio. Jan and I knew several people who'd gone to the retreat and highly recommended it. I began saying, "What If?—What if we go to this silent retreat to find the purpose of our being together?" To this day, I'm not sure how I talked Jan into it, but we went.

We were, however, allowed to talk during dinner the first evening. Afterward, a little white-haired man (who I'm sure was one of the original apostles) came up to us and said, "You're our married couple." Jan and I looked at each other and thought, "What have we gotten into?"

We gathered in another room, where each person stood up one by one and shared why they were there and what they hoped to gain from the retreat. After listening to everyone's stories, we realized what was happening. We were the only two people who weren't preparing to be a priest, a nun, or a missionary. Our friends who'd recommended this retreat forgot to share this part with us! We each struggled to voice why we were there. Quite frankly, I don't think we knew.

Since it was a silent retreat, Jan and I had separate rooms. I'd get up in the morning and, at breakfast, I'd look at the person across from me and wonder what their story was, but I couldn't speak. But we could attend a group exercise class or a morning devotional, where it was nice to hear someone talking.

We were each assigned a spiritual director, and we met together for an hour a day. Jan (my ADHD husband) was assigned to be with a nun, and she wanted to teach him how to be centered through quietness and meditation. (All right, he might not have Attention Deficit Hyperactivity Disorder, but his attention span is a little short!) She told him to visualize himself in a canoe that was drifting down the river. She told him to simply be quiet and let everything float by. If debris floated by, he was not to get out of the canoe to chase it. She suggested that he sit and meditate and try to access a quiet place inside him.

My spiritual director was probably the only layperson in this role, and she'd also been married and divorced. It didn't take her long to understand who I was. She told me to calm down and enjoy the journey. She said that I had to quit moving so fast—to enjoy life and quit trying to make everything happen.

> *She told me to calm down and enjoy the journey. She said that I had to quit moving so fast—to enjoy life and quit trying to make everything happen.*

We were supposed to stay on the grounds of the retreat center, but she gave me permission to go for a walk in the back of the property. She said that if I kept walking, I'd reach a small town. She suggested that I stroll around, enjoy the day, have a cup of coffee, and do a little shopping. How freeing it was to just be. I didn't have to do *anything*.

The next day, I told her what I'd done and how liberating it was. She said, "That's great! Today, we have someone coming into the center to give massages to anyone who's interested. You may want to try it." Wow! I liked this suggestion even more.

Since Jan and I were a married couple, we were allowed to meet after dinner to discuss what our day had been like. This became our evening ritual. Jan talked about what he did that day to learn to be quiet and meditate, and I told him I'd walked into town for a cup of coffee.

Around the third or fourth day into the retreat, my spiritual director asked me if I ever skipped. I laughed and said, "Yes, when I was five."

"You should try skipping," she said. "You can't be in a hurry when you skip. You can't be angry when you skip. You're just happy."

Because she wanted me to get in touch with the little girl who liked to play, she proposed that I go out on the retreat grounds, pick a flower, put it in my hair, and then skip through the property. So that's exactly what I did! At that exact moment, Jan was meeting with his spiritual director, and she was trying to get him to be quiet and meditate. When he looked out the window, guess what he saw? You guessed it; he saw me picking a flower from a tree, putting it in my hair, and skipping off through the woods!

> Because she wanted me to get in touch with the little girl who liked to play, she proposed that I go out on the retreat grounds, pick a flower, put it in my hair, and then skip through the property.

On our last visit, my spiritual director said, "I usually give someone a card and a cross or something as a reminder to help them on their journey." With that, she gave me a giant wand to blow bubbles and told me to learn to play and be happy.

To this day, we still laugh about the things we did at this retreat. I actually think it was a greater experience of growth and unity in our marriage than we realized at the time. It was certainly a shared experience. I sometimes wonder if God is asking us to just be, not do.

What is meditation? While mediation can be different for different people, learning to meditate was a process for me. I once took a meditation class where the facilitator told us to buy a single rose. We were then to go home and stare at the rose petals as we sat in complete silence. The idea was to learn to sit in silence and to be comfortable with it.

Once you're comfortable sitting in silence, you simply take deep breaths and concentrate on your breathing, letting your thoughts come and go. When you first try to do this, you'll be overwhelmed with thoughts: things you need to do, things you didn't do, and things you want to do. Just as Jan learned at the silent retreat, try imagining yourself in a canoe drifting down the river. Logs will float by, much like your thoughts, but you just let them float by rather than jumping out of the canoe and chasing after them.

You may say, "I can't just sit and be quiet. You don't know how busy I am," or, "I'm afraid of my thoughts." I understand because I thought the same thing. But in this busy, negative world, where more and more people experience anxiety and panic attacks, isn't it worth a try to calm your mind?

Meditation isn't for everyone. Some people find quiet by walking in nature. Others have so much going on in their heads that they can't be left alone with their thoughts. I had this problem when I was so horribly ill after I was diagnosed with cancer. I was overwhelmed and was having panic attacks. I couldn't get to a place of peace by myself. So, I meditated by listening to guided meditations, where someone else spoke words of affirmation and healing over me.

EXERCISE: CHAPTER 7

- What would help you to meditate?
- Choose a quiet, calm place to begin meditating.
- Would it help you to stare at a rose or some other object?
- Remember to take deep breaths ... in and out.
- Let your thoughts float by; just concentrate on your breathing.

CHAPTER 8

Life After Marriage

*"The future belongs to those who believe in the
beauty of their dreams."*

~ Eleanor Roosevelt

I'd married Jan and moved to a new town. But now what? What would I do with my time? I certainly wasn't ready to retire. I tried selling Arbonne skin care products and put a team together with my daughter for a while, but there wasn't a synchronicity and the flow wasn't right, so I knew it was time to do something else.

And yet, it's clear that Arbonne came into my life for a reason. First, it was an opportunity to work with my daughter, and I met other wonderful people who would later be influential in my life. Second, selling Arbonne was my introduction to searching for new ways toward health and wellness. Arbonne's products are plant-based, which I learned had great health benefits, considering that these products are absorbed into one of our largest organs, the skin.

Around this time, Jan and I learned about Klemmer and Associates, which offered a Personal Mastery weekend that we attended in Chicago. The weekend was great. We did several exercises that took us out of our "boxes" and showed us that there were different ways of doing things. If anyone needed to learn how to do things differently, it was the two of us. The weekend was very useful and gave us a lot to talk about.

Then came the sales pitch. They were offering an advanced five-day leadership program in California. If you signed up that weekend, the price would be reduced. This program promised to take you to the next level; the sunglasses would come off and you would see the world in a new light. I was in. I was between careers at the time and knew that if I kept searching, I'd find out what to do next. I talked to Jan about it, and he agreed to go.

The first evening, we walked around the room and talked to each person and told them a little bit about ourselves. I don't remember a lot about it, but I do remember that some of the attendees disagreed with one another. At the end of the evening, we were instructed to tell someone what we didn't like about them. I knew things were going south at this point, but by then we'd already bought in. Some people became quite vocal about what they didn't like about the other person. I realized that if I didn't pick someone fast, I'd be picked by some bully I couldn't stand up to.

Ironically, many of us found that we'd picked the person who was the mirror image of ourselves. The part we didn't like about that person was a reflection of our own self.

So I walked up to a sweet lady and said, "I don't like that you are so quiet and shy, and you let people walk all over you." I'm not proud of that moment, but I later came to respect this woman. She's a well-loved and respected woman who would never walk up to someone and tell them what she didn't like about them. Yikes!

Ironically, many of us found that we'd picked the person who was the mirror image of ourselves. The part we didn't like about that person was a reflection of our own self. As it turned out, the person you didn't like became your buddy for the next five days.

Parts of this experience were thought-provoking and life-changing. However, I'm not a believer in the means justifying the end. I don't think people have to be beaten up in order to learn. While that approach works for some people, it's not for me. It was like a military approach: beat people down and then build them back up. In the end, I felt pretty beat up for the next five days and for quite a while afterward. We were yelled at, made fun of, and not allowed to have water in the meeting room, which, by the way, was cold enough to make you wish you'd brought a winter coat.

However, I did things I never thought I'd do, like climb to the top of a telephone pole in a redwood forest and climb forty feet in the air on a ladder attached to a tree. From there, I walked out on a tightrope that was made of something that appeared to be a garden hose. Of course, I was harnessed up and belayed. I'd never done anything like this before, so it was hard to believe that someone would catch me when I fell.

I climbed to the top of the telephone pole and got only one foot on top. I couldn't for the life of me get my second foot on top of the telephone pole and stand straight up in the time allotted. They questioned me, asking where else I wasn't getting to the top. I felt like a failure.

Then came the next test. This time, my buddy and I were a team. We were again harnessed up and belayed, and we stood side by side, each facing a forty-foot tree with wooden slats attached to it in the form of a ladder. We each had to get to the top and then step out onto parallel tightwires or tightropes. I was bound and determined to accomplish this challenge.

As I raced up the ladder, I heard my name being called. I was told to come back down, where I saw my buddy near the bottom. When I got down, she said, "I can't do this." I told her we'd do it together and that I'd learned to do this in other areas of my life.

"You can't look up or down," I said. "Just look at each step as you're taking it and believe that you can take that one step."

We finally made it to the top, but she was afraid to walk out on the tightrope for fear of falling. This time as I tried to reassure her, my words didn't even sound believable to me.

"Look, we're going to walk out on the rope and hold on to each other," I said. We're belayed, and there's no way down other than falling. We can be afraid and fall, or we can go out there and help each other walk across."

I'm incredibly proud that my buddy and I walked out on those parallel ropes. As we held on to each other, the farther we went out, the further apart our ropes separated from one another, causing us to lean in closer with each step. We had a blind faith, knowing that we were belayed and that if we fell, we'd be lowered to the ground unharmed.

Eager to start something new, I earned my real estate license and started selling real estate. I knew I didn't want to work nights and weekends like I'd done in the past, so I joined a team and worked under someone else. Once again, I questioned if I'd done the right thing by leaving State Farm. But I know that this was where I needed to be. I met some wonderful people who will be my friends for life, and the experience allowed me to make investments that helped me save for retirement.

I've always been a dreamer. I'd say to Jan, "What if?" This time, I asked, "What if we could buy rental property to help us build our retirement package?" Over time, Jan learned to cringe at the words, "What if?"

Buying rental property was, once again, a stretch for me. I bought a book called *HOLD: How to Find, Buy, and Rent Houses for Wealth*. It's the best book I've read on buying and renting real estate. It stressed the importance of buying the same kind of properties and detailed how to look for properties that would provide a good cash flow. It also had some great suggestions on how to finance the purchases if you didn't pay cash. As a realtor, I had access to our local Multiple Listing Service (MLS) and was able to research properties that were coming on the market. I'd spend hours doing the math to see what type of properties would work for us. Once I had a plan in place, the project took on a life of its own. Again, it was a time of synchronicity in my life.

Finding and buying houses was one thing. But now we had to rent them and keep them rented. We had a little experience with this work, since we'd previously bought our retirement home and rented it out in the winter. While the Arizona home was in a different rental market, we faced a lot of the same issues. We've been blessed with great renters. Although we've had the occasional "oops," it has been a positive experience overall.

There was a lot to consider as we merged our two lives together. Some of it was exciting. Some of it was not so exciting;

> There was a lot to consider as we merged our two lives together. Some of it was exciting. Some of it was not so exciting; it was just plain hard work.

it was just plain hard work. Jan was the rock, and he kept doing a great job with his business, while I tried to decide what I wanted to be when I grew up.

EXERCISE: CHAPTER 8

Do you allow yourself to dream? What do you want to be? What do you want to have? What do you want to do? If you're going to have the life you want, you need to start with the end in mind. Now that you know the improvements you want to make in the six key areas of life, let's get started.

- Get a notebook and list one hundred things you want to be, do, or have. Do this step quickly. Find a quiet place and allow only twenty minutes for the task. Don't think about it; just start writing. Let it flow. At this point, nothing is too simple or too far out. And guess what? These are now your goals.
- Next, begin with the end in mind. Think about what you want your tombstone to say. On your tombstone might be the date you were born - - - and the date you died. What's the dash, dash, dash inside of those dates going to say about you? Or, consider if you'll wish you had done things differently at the end of your life. Will you have regrets? Or will you be happy with what you have? If you envision yourself being happy, what will you have accomplished?
- Next, with your list of one hundred goals in front of you, write down your six-year vision. What do you want your life to look like in six years? Describe your vision in the present tense. What does it look like, smell like,

taste like, and feel like? What are you doing, where are you living, and who are you with?

- Create a vision board by cutting pictures out of magazines to represent what you want to be, do, and have. Glue these pictures on a poster board, which will be a daily visual reminder of your goals. While you might find it especially helpful to complete this project in a group workshop, you can do it on your own.

CHAPTER 9

Retirement—The Grand Life

"Goals. There's no telling what you can do when you get inspired by them. There's no telling what you can do when you believe in them. And there's no telling what will happen when you act upon them."

~ Jim Rohn

had visualized my retirement for years. When I described my six-year vision, I saw myself sitting on my Arizona patio with a cup of coffee in the morning and a glass of wine at sunset. I visualized golfing several times a week, being in a book club, entertaining, traveling, and just relaxing.

I retired at the end of 2016, and that's exactly what I did. What a life! I spent the rest of the winter in my home in Arizona. I became sick twice that winter, but both times I was told I had bronchitis. However, it was like no bronchitis I'd ever had before.

On April 2, 2017, I became sick again. This time I was in Arizona by myself, and I knew I was incredibly ill. I woke up thinking I needed to get to an Urgent Care. I could have called several people who would've been happy to drive me, but I wanted to drive myself. I didn't know what I had, and I didn't want to give it to anyone else. As I lay in bed waking up, this thought kept coming to my mind: *They meant it for evil, but I meant it for good*. And then I'd recall the Bible verse, "For I know the plans I have for you,' declares the Lord, 'plans to prosper you and not to harm you, plans to give you hope and a future" (Jeremiah 29:11 NIV). The second verse had been a positive affirmation in my life for a long time, but the first one, "They meant it for evil, but I meant it for good," wasn't. In the following months, I clung to these two verses and repeated them as my mantra.

> As I lay in bed waking up, this thought kept coming to my mind: They meant it for evil, but I meant it for good.

Jan and I had plans to take a trip out of the country, so I needed to fly back to Illinois. I made an appointment at the clinic back in Champaign for April 6. My doctor had retired the year before, so I was directed to see a nurse practitioner. This appointment began my hellacious journey of falling through the cracks in the local medical community.

The nurse practitioner examined me, gave me medication, and ordered chest x-rays, which showed something in my lungs. She then ordered additional x-rays to be taken two weeks later. Meanwhile, I got sicker. Our friends in Arizona told Jan that I should be tested for Valley Fever, since I'd spent the winter there. The clinic agreed, and when I went to have my blood drawn, I was so weak I couldn't walk back to the lab. I had to be pushed in a wheelchair. When the nurse practitioner saw me waiting in the wheelchair, she patted me on the arm and told me I'd be fine. She didn't order any additional blood work, which would have shown exactly what I had.

Two weeks later, the follow-up chest x-ray revealed collapsed air sacs in my left lung, as well as hyperinflation comparable to Chronic Obstructive Pulmonary Disease in both lungs. Finally, the nurse practitioner referred me to a pulmonary specialist, and I waited three weeks for that appointment. The pulmonary specialist ran some tests then concluded that I had asthma and told me to come back in a year for a recheck. It seemed like the doctors were all done with me, but I kept getting sicker.

By now, I started having panic attacks. I wasn't sleeping at night and could only sleep for a couple of hours at a time during the day. I continued to go for walks; I thought that if I kept exercising, I'd get strong and healthy again. Some days I'd walk for two miles until I felt like my legs would give out. Then for the next two or three days, I couldn't get out of bed.

I had no idea what was wrong with me. I thought it was a bad flu

> I had no idea what was wrong with me. I thought it was a bad flu that I just couldn't shake.

that I just couldn't shake. My system was shutting down, I'd lost a lot of weight, and my muscles were being eaten up by the disease. I not only had panic attacks; I was paranoid. I was a loose cannon, blasting at everyone around me. My children kept their distance, tired of my lashing out and the comments I'd make. I couldn't stand any noise and sat in a chair in my room by myself for hours in a way that bore no resemblance to my formerly active life. Friends called me, but I didn't have the energy to return their calls. A couple of friends stopped by and saw the state I was in. None of us had a clue about what was to happen.

I'd started to see a therapist, because I was not only physically ill, I was also mentally and emotionally exhausted. Although the rest of the medical community had written me off, my therapist encouraged me to keep looking for the cause of my illness. She suggested that I see a cardiologist since I felt like I wasn't getting enough oxygen and was having trouble breathing. I had also had a silent heart attack years earlier.

I called the cardiology department of the local hospital and was told I needed a referral before I could be seen. Next, I called the office of my pulmonary specialist and learned that he didn't make referrals. I'd have to go back to my primary care doctor. So I called the nurse practitioner, but learned that since she wasn't my doctor, I'd have to make an appointment with a new primary care doctor. I set an appointment for June 8.

The new doctor looked at my chart and said she saw no reason to refer me to a cardiologist. She told me I had emphysema, yet nowhere on my chart did it say anything about emphysema. When I challenged her, she became angry and said, "Do you want me to examine you or do you want to leave right now?" I told her to go ahead and examine me. She finally said she'd refer me to a cardiologist, so he could tell me there was nothing wrong with me. She noticed that it had been a while since I'd had blood work, so she wrote an order to have this work done.

Jan had been at the appointment with me, and later that evening he innocently asked, "What's inside of you that you had to argue with the doctor?"

I immediately became unglued and responded, "It's *my* freakin' body!"

Jan and I have talked a lot about this conversation since that day, and I asked his permission to tell this story. But this story goes well beyond Jan. Isn't this how we've all been conditioned to think—that we shouldn't argue with a doctor? After all, they know much more about medicine than we do. But does every doctor have our best interests at heart? Because of what I've been through, I would say, "Absolutely *not!*" It's up to each of us to listen to our bodies, to hear the still, small voice inside, and determine what's right for us. Don't let someone else tell you what's right for you—not even a doctor, particularly if you question their sincerity.

The next morning, I went to the clinic to have my blood work done. At noon, the phone rang. It was the same doctor who'd practically thrown me out of her office the day before. She said, "We have your blood work back, and your white blood cell count is extremely high. You need to see a hematologist right away." She said she'd contact a hematologist to set up an appointment and would call me back.

Within an hour, she called back to tell me that because my white cell count was extremely high, the hematologist didn't want me to wait for an appointment. He, instead, directed me to go to the emergency room immediately. She told me—over the phone—that I had leukemia and that the hematologist would call the emergency room doctor to tell him or her how to do a bone marrow biopsy.

She insisted again that I leave immediately for the emergency room, and I told her I had to process this news and talk to my husband. My still, small voice was saying, "There has to be a better way." This same doctor called my cell phone

> *She told me—over the phone— that I had leukemia and that the hematologist would call the emergency room doctor to tell him or her how to do a bone marrow biopsy.*

four times that afternoon and Jan's four times as well, and she left messages that said how important it was for me to get to the emergency room immediately.

It was a Friday afternoon, and I decided to wait until I saw the blood work myself and could get a second opinion. I was in total shock. Normal white blood cell counts should be between 4,000 and 11,000 per microliter. Mine was 267,000. I was later told that I probably had six weeks to live. It had been two months since I'd originally gone to the doctor because of my cough, and now I found out I had cancer.

How could this be? Hadn't I gone from doctor to doctor for those two months and told them how sick I was? This couldn't be happening to me. It must be someone else. Cancer? I couldn't have cancer.

That's when I decided to get a second opinion.

EXERCISE: CHAPTER 9

If I hadn't learned to set goals earlier in my life, I couldn't have visualized my healing or believed that I was healed. My process of goal setting and discipline was put to the test as I once again learned to meditate and to repeat the disciplines I'd learned earlier. I knew my life would depend on prayer, believing I was healed, exercising when I didn't feel like I could, and learning a new way of eating, along with integrative treatments that would heal and detoxify me from the cancer.

Because goal setting is so important to me, I've added a section on setting smart goals. Smart goals can be defined in the following way:

S – Specific
M – Measurable

A – Achievable

R – Relevant

T – Time Sensitive

Ask yourself the following questions:

- Specific: What do I want to accomplish and why?
- Measurable: How much and by when? How will I know when the goal is accomplished?
- Achievable: How can I accomplish this goal? Even if it's a stretch, is it realistic?
- Relevant: Does this goal make sense? Do I really want to accomplish it? (Remember—this goal is yours, not something someone else wants you to do. Will accomplishing this goal excite you?)
- Time Sensitive: When will I accomplish this goal? In six days, six weeks, six months, or six years?

Think back to the one hundred goals you wrote down. What would you really like to be, do, and have? Are you willing to claim these goals and work for them? If they're large goals, break them down into smaller steps that lead you to the larger goals. What obstacles might get in the way? Time, money, people? How will you overcome these obstacles? How will you motivate yourself? Are you disciplined enough on your own, or do you need an accountability partner or a life coach?

How will these goals fit into your day? Try to block time during each hour of the day for specific tasks that need to be done to get you to your goal.

Write a SMART goal in each of the six areas of your life, using the worksheet on the next page.

GOAL WORKSHEET

Goal: _____

Obstacle: _____

How will you know this is accomplished?

_____

When: _____

What tasks do I need to complete to reach this goal? How frequently do I need to do each task—Daily? Weekly? Or at some other frequency?

CHAPTER 10

_____

The Search for New Doctors

"Whether you think you can or think you can't, you're right."

~ Henry Ford

I'd fallen through the cracks in the local medical community, but God had another plan for me. I was so sick between April and June that I didn't know where to turn. A friend of mine suggested I see a doctor in Aurora, Illinois who offered alternative medical treatments.

GOD WINK #1

I'd already made an appointment three weeks earlier and, as God would have it, the appointment was set for the Wednesday following my diagnosis. This doctor did more blood work and verified that I did, indeed, have leukemia. I'd been so sure she was going to tell me the blood work had been a mistake and that I didn't have leukemia that I was once again in shock. I asked her about her alternative treatments, and she said my disease was too far along for that. I'd need to see a hematologist and undergo conventional treatment. She suggested I see Dr. Keith Block at the Block Center for Integrative Cancer Treatment in Skokie, Illinois.

The next day was Thursday, and I researched the Block Center online. On Friday, I called to make an appointment and spoke to a patient advocate, who said they needed the paperwork and lab work from my previous doctors. I also needed to fill out a fourteen-page questionnaire before they could see me. She said it usually took thirty days to get an appointment. I told her my situation and explained I couldn't wait that long.

GOD WINK #2

The patient advocate put me on hold, then told me that Dr. Block had a cancellation at 9:00 a.m. on Monday morning. Could I be there? Of course, the answer was yes.

Jan and my daughter Melissa went with me to help me assimilate all the information I'd receive. We met with Dr. Block and the representatives from each integrative department. I underwent assessments that lasted from 9:00 a.m. until 6:00 p.m.

Dr. Block and his team walked us through all the things I'd have to do in order to heal. First, I'd have to meditate and actually *believe* that I was healed. I'd have to change my diet and take supplements that supported the healing process. I'd need to exercise and keep moving, even when I didn't feel like it. Most important, I'd have monthly infusions to build up my body, not only from the disease, but also from the drugs that treat the disease. These infusions would consist of vitamins and nutrients, glutathione, vitamin C, and curcumin.

First, I'd have to meditate and actually believe that I was healed.

I didn't know that treatments like these existed in the United States. We researched them all online and discovered their benefits. Why hadn't we known about these treatments? When I found Dr. Block, I finally found a doctor who cared about me as a whole person.

GOD WINK #3

While we were still at the center, Dr. Block called Dr. Jayesh Mehta, the Director of the Stem Cell Therapy Department at Northwestern Medical Center in Chicago, and asked him to see me as a patient. Dr. Mehta knew the targeted drug and the dosage I should be on for Chronic Myelogenous Leukemia, the kind of leukemia I have. However, Dr. Mehta couldn't prescribe it for me until he could see me at Northwestern, and I couldn't get an appointment right away. Dr. Block and Dr. Mehta agreed that I should go back to my local hospital to ask if a hematologist would prescribe this drug, since time was of the essence and it would take me a while to get an appointment with Dr. Mehta.

I made an appointment with a hematologist at our local hospital, and Jan and my daughter Jodi went with me. The hematologist told us that she wouldn't work with Dr. Block and she wouldn't use a targeted drug; she only used liquid chemo. I asked if she would talk to the other hematologists in the hospital to see if any of them would work with me. Several days later, someone from the hospital called to tell me that none of the hematologists would work with Dr. Block, and that none of them would use a targeted drug. So I waited for my appointment with Dr. Mehta.

As it turned out, I got to see Dr. Block and had an appointment with Dr. Mehta within ten days of being diagnosed. God was truly at work. But while I waited to see Dr. Block and Dr. Mehta, some of my children weren't happy with me because I didn't go to the emergency room to get hooked up to chemo.

"Why aren't you doing what the doctor told you to do?" they asked.

Sometimes you have to be quiet and listen to the still, small voice inside. I knew my children were just as frightened as I was. They were simply processing my diagnosis differently.

When I was first diagnosed, I was in shock. Then I felt disbelief and thought they must be talking about someone else—not me. I thought that if they did another blood test, it would be normal. My mind raced. Maybe it was all a mistake. While I was waiting to get in to see Dr. Mehta, I finally came to terms with the fact that I had cancer. I decided that I'd been through many journeys in life and that God had always walked alongside me or led me when I needed it the most. Cancer would be yet another journey.

> I decided that I'd been through many journeys in life and that God had always walked alongside me or led me when I needed it the most. Cancer would be yet another journey.

I now had a new goal: to become healthy. How would I do that? What would it look like? I started calling people who cared about me to asked them to pray for my healing. I chose to believe God had the answers and that I had to give it to Him—not part of it, but all of it. I had a blind faith, but I also had nowhere else to turn.

I talked to Jan about the power of prayer and asked if he believed that God could heal me. We discussed it at length, and I asked if we could pray together and if he would pray over me. Anyone who knows Jan knows that he's very soft-spoken. Yet, when he started praying, it was as if he was speaking with a different voice. He commanded every cancer cell to leave my body and then began thanking God that I'd already been healed. I'd heard powerful prayers before, but none as powerful as this one. Afterward, we looked at each other, and in that moment, I knew I'd been healed.

I meditated every morning when I got out of bed. I couldn't be still and meditate on my own because there was too much noise going on in my head, so I listened to music that affirmed and inspired me and that helped me visualize my healing.

GOD WINK #4

Shortly after Jan's prayer, my appointment with Dr. Mehta was moved up. We were impressed with both Dr. Mehta and Northwestern. He's an extremely busy man, and yet he had time to answer our questions. He was compassionate and caring.

Within four weeks of seeing Dr. Mehta and starting the targeted drug—as well as receiving infusions from Dr. Block—my white blood cell count fell down into the normal range. As elated as we were, I still had a long recovery ahead of me.

We had a lot to learn as we researched what a targeted drug was, and we learned the following from the National Cancer Institute:

Targeted cancer therapies are drugs or other substances that block the growth and spread of cancer by interfering with specific molecules ("molecular targets") that are involved in the growth, progression, and spread of cancer. Targeted cancer therapies are sometimes called "molecularly targeted drugs," "molecularly targeted therapies," "precision medicines," or similar names.

Targeted therapies differ from standard chemotherapy in several ways:

- Targeted therapies act on specific molecular targets that are associated with cancer, whereas most standard chemotherapies act on all rapidly dividing normal and cancerous cells.

- Targeted therapies are deliberately chosen or designed to interact with their target, whereas many standard chemotherapies were identified because they kill cells.

- Targeted therapies are often cytostatic (that is, they block tumor cell proliferation), whereas standard chemotherapy agents are cytotoxic (that is, they kill tumor cells).

When I started taking the drug, I was afraid because I didn't know what to expect. For an hour in the morning and again in the evening after taking the drug, I listened to calming music and visualized my healing. During those mornings, I thought about all the discipline I'd learned from coaching with Dr. Tom Hill. Dr. Block told me that I was in the top ten percent of his patients—and that I was probably in the top one percent of patients—who practiced everything he asked me to do. I believed these habits could be traced to the discipline I'd already learned regarding diet, exercise, visualization, and meditation—habits I'd learned many years before. I actually believed I could be healed.

I'd lost so much weight by then that I had trouble walking without losing my balance. A friend asked me what kind of help I needed, but I didn't know how to answer. She talked to Jan, and they decided that since I needed someone to be with me at all times, they would put together a schedule of people who would come in to help me on Tuesdays and Thursdays. That way, Jan could meet clients and do the things he needed to do for work. My daughter Melissa had a list of people who wanted updates on my progress, so she sent the schedule to them. These friends showed up every Tuesday and Thursday for as long as I needed to take me for walks, to get lunch, or to do whatever needed to be done so that Jan could go to work.

I'm in awe of the people who showed up to help me in this way, as well as those who sent cards, emails, and texts to let me know how much they cared about me and that they were praying for me. I still become emotional when I think about it.

We all need one another. Life is not meant to be lived alone.

We all need one another. Life is not meant to be lived alone. Quite frankly, I'd gotten pretty good over the years saying something like, "If I can do anything, let me know." But these individuals instead said to me, "We're going to walk this journey with you."

EXERCISE: CHAPTER 10

Jim Rohn once said, "You are the average of the five people you spend the most time with." Who do you spend time with, and who influences what you think and do? Rohn also said, "Success leaves clues." Find people who've done what you want to do and learn from them. You can emulate these individuals to achieve your goals in each of the six areas of your life.

You can also start your own mastermind group, as described by Napoleon Hill in the book *Think and Grow Rich*. Invite high-achieving people to be part of the group, then ask each of them to invite one other person. Hill notes that the beauty of a mastermind group is that the members can challenge one another to create or implement goals.

If you can't form a group, at least find an accountability partner or a life coach who can challenge you and keep you accountable to work toward your goals. Although I was adept at setting professional goals, I needed a life coach to help me set and meet goals in all the other areas of my life.

Who will walk alongside you and be an advocate for you when you're in a crisis? I was blessed to have a group of family and friends that came in and helped me when I was too sick to do so.

- What will you do to find out more about mastermind groups?
- Who will you ask to be in your mastermind group?
- What focus do you want your mastermind group to have?
- When will you do this?

CHAPTER 11

Sharing My Story

"A time to tear and a time to mend, a time to be silent and a time to speak."

~ Ecclesiastes 3:7 (NIV)

N ow I want to ask the question, *Why did this happen to me?* from a different perspective. Life is truly a gift; it's not to be taken for granted. So how can I use this gift to help others?

If I didn't know that integrative cancer treatments existed, then how many other people don't know about them? Of course, there are some who don't want to know. They think there's only the conventional way of treating the disease, and they won't try anything else. Then there are others who will tuck this information away and, when they or a loved one are in a crisis, they'll already know there are alternatives. Then there's a third group of people who are ready to hear about integrative cancer treatment now.

All my life, I've tried alternative medicine when given a choice. I always believed that if I ever had cancer, I'd choose an alternative treatment. However, when faced with it, I had no idea what to do or where to turn. I didn't know anyone who'd traveled to Mexico or somewhere other than the United States for treatment. Since then, I've talked to people who've traveled for treatment and others who've been healed by alternative treatments. At the Block Center, I found an integrative approach that combined conventional and alternative treatments. There are many more options out there, and I will continue to search for them.

> *I always believed that if I ever had cancer, I'd choose an alternative treatment. However, when faced with it, I had no idea what to do or where to turn.*

I'm certain that God led me to Dr. Block and Dr. Mehta. Although I'm taking a drug, I'm blessed to have found integrative treatment that would restore me to health. I've talked to many patients at the Block Center who have amazing stories. Their stories, as well as information about Keith and Penny Block, can be found on the Block Center website. Dr. Block has also authored a book, *Life Over Cancer*. If you're serious about knowing more, it's a must-read.

It's been two and a half years since I started treatments, and I've come so far since then. People ask me if I'm back to normal, but the truth is that I'll never be the person I was before. I'm now living a *new* normal. Healing is a day-by-day process, and I'm elated to be at this point in my life. I'm not considered to be in remission, but I am close.

I now realize that I'd been sick for many years before I was diagnosed with leukemia. Six years earlier, I'd gone to the emergency room with chest pains and stomach problems. After a battery of tests, the doctors told me they didn't know what was wrong, but that they suspected it was my gallbladder. They suggested that I follow up with my primary care physician, which I did. She wanted to remove my gallbladder, but since the emergency room doctor wasn't sure that my gallbladder was the problem, I didn't want to do that. When I told my doctor, she said, "Ouch! You just want to wait to see if this happens again?"

Over the next few years, I saw many doctors, and even took two trips to the Mayo Clinic to determine the problem. The doctors at Mayo told me there was nothing wrong with my gallbladder, but neither could they find the cause of my discomfort. My health continued to decline, and I was told it was because I was getting older. But now, the integrative treatment I've chosen—which includes IV infusions, supplements, diet, and exercise—has restored my body back to health. I believe that I've been healed.

I often think about the day when the doctor called, told me that I had leukemia, and said to go the emergency room immediately. How many people are coerced into treatments they don't want because they're afraid? What's happened to our medical system? Is it broken—or is it more sinister than that? Why do we force people into chemo and radiation when so many of them will die from the poison that's put in their bodies? The medical system tries to make us think we don't have options, and it's a frightening situation.

It may be hard for you to believe me when I tell you about my success using an integrative approach. My advice is to do your own research. Find out for yourself how many people are being helped by chemo and radiation, as well as how many people die from these treatments. A couple of years ago, I wouldn't have said such harsh things, but having lived in the system for the past two years, I've seen some very frightening things. I believe that if I'd been hooked up to liquid chemo, I would have died.

> My advice is to do your own research. Find out for yourself how many people are being helped by chemo and radiation, as well as how many people die from these treatments.

I watched a video series, *The Truth About Cancer: A Global Quest*, and these radical videos have opened my eyes to what's happening with cancer treatments—not only in the United States, but globally. I don't know that I would've been totally open to the ideas presented in the videos if I hadn't lived through my own hellacious journey in our health care system. I encourage you to watch these videos, which include a great deal of information about what we can do to prevent and cure cancer.

I also viewed a documentary called *The C Word*. I was very touched by this film and the amount of information it provided. There's a lot of statistical data in it regarding areas we're never told about. I encourage anyone who wants more information to watch this film.

I well remember that day in April 2017, when I woke up terribly ill and heard the words, "They meant it for evil, but I meant it for good." At the time, I didn't know where this verse came from, but I've since learned it's from Genesis: "But as for you, you meant evil against me; but God meant it for good, in order to bring it about as it is to this day, to save many people alive" (Genesis 50:20 NKJV).

What does this verse mean? At first, I thought it might refer to my experience of falling through the cracks in the medical community before I found the right doctors. Or maybe it was that I saw first-hand the horrible treatments that are inflicted on patients but then found my way with integrative treatment. I wonder if the cancer in my body is helping me find true peace and complete surrender. The truth is that I don't know and will never know for sure. But one thing I *do* know is that it's a daily walk by faith, and I will share my story in hopes of helping others.

> *The truth is that I don't know and will never know for sure. But one thing I do know is that it's a daily walk by faith ...*

My advice is to find a specialist, ask questions, and get a second opinion—and a third and fourth if necessary. Make sure you know what each procedure entails, what the expected recovery time is, and what you'll have to endure to get there. Make educated decisions; don't just follow what someone else is telling you. It's your body. You have options. Listen to the still, small voice inside.

My decision to go to Dr. Block changed my life. I don't pretend to have all the answers, but I know that the mainstream cancer treatment isn't working. I will continue to search for even more answers, as I hope you will.

When faced with a crisis:

- Follow your daily disciplines.
- Be quiet and listen to the still, small voice inside. Don't follow the herd.
- Be open to God Winks, or to the moments when God shows up in your life.
- Do some due diligence before you are in a crisis and learn more about treatment alternatives.

EXERCISE: CHAPTER 11

SHARING MY OWN GOALS

I'm going to share a little about how I set my own goals and what's important to me, bearing in mind that we all have different goals and will rank the different areas of our lives in our own order.

The two most important areas to me are *spiritual* and *health*. For a long time, I didn't think that health should rank second because I had so many responsibilities and so many other people to take care of. But I realized that if I didn't attend to my health, I'd be no good for anyone else. So here are my goals:

- Spiritual: To me this means being at peace with God. I achieve this peace by doing the following:
  □ Reading
  □ Praying
  □ Meditating
  □ Attending church
  □ Walking in nature
- Health: This has ranked second for me for a while now, but I didn't know it was that important until I became ill. It soon became apparent that I had to give everything to God, and from there I had one goal: to be healthy.
  □ Diet—My diet is pretty much a vegan diet with cold-water fish a couple of times a week. I eat organic when possible and stay away from processed sugar.

    To convey the benefit of eating organic food, I'll tell you a story. I have a brother who bought farmland over the years. The more land he bought, the more he planted organic crops. One day, I asked him how he started this process and his answer surprised me. When he was a young man and helping our father farm, they didn't use pesticides or commercial fertilizers. He learned to farm organically by farming with Dad. Could it be that simple? I asked my husband Jan, who's a farm manager, about that. He said pesticides and commercial fertilizers weren't used until the 1940s, and when my father was farming in North Dakota, he was probably still rotating crops and not using pesticides. My mother's garden also would've been organic. While you may not believe in eating organically grown food, it's what we all ate at one time.

If eating organic doesn't throw you off, a vegan diet may do so. In all honesty, I'd tried to eat vegan once before in my life. It was the book *The China Study*, which includes research on how animal protein feeds cancer, that convinced me. I think that when I ate a vegan diet before, I replaced meat and dairy with too many processed foods. But when I was diagnosed with cancer, I saw the importance of implementing a healthier vegan diet.

If my advice to eat an organic and vegan diet doesn't throw you off, I'm sure some of you may have a hard time giving up sugar, but I believe it's worth it.

- Exercise—My exercise consists of a combination of yoga, walking, and biking six days a week. I've always exercised, but after working with Dr. Block I knew it would become an even bigger part of my life.

▫ Rest—The need for rest is too often overlooked in our busy world. When I was growing up, no one worked on Sundays and no stores were open, so you couldn't go shopping or run out for groceries. We'd go to church and afterward, we'd either visit with relatives or go home and have dinner as a family. Then we took naps. As a child, I thought that Sundays were boring and that when I grew up, I'd find something fun to do. Over the years, I've had the opportunity to do just that. However, I've come full circle, and now I need that day of quiet and rest. I'm at a different place in my life; I don't have children at home who are involved in all kinds of activities. Find a day—it doesn't have to be a Sunday—when you can slow down and rest, unplug from what's stressing you out, and just learn to be at peace. Do something that works for you. It can be yoga or a walk—anything that will slow you down and help you find peace.

CHAPTER 12

Questions Along the Way

"What you get by achieving your goals is not as important as what you become by achieving your goals."

~ Zig Ziglar

E ver since I was diagnosed with cancer, I've been asked a lot of questions about what I did to get healthy. Often when I'm speaking to someone who's recently been diagnosed, they say, "I've given it to God, and if it's His will, I'll be healed." This concept is hard for me to understand. What's my part and what's God's part? Does God expect us to be doormats when it comes to our health and simply surrender? Or does He expect us to seek and find the answers that are right for us?

Why do we so often choose to say it's God's will when we're ill? When we're raising children, it's our responsibility to make sure they're learning and not being taken advantage of. We don't let them run in the street and then say that if it's God's will, they'll stay healthy. No, we make sure we're doing everything we can to raise healthy and safe children. Why wouldn't we do the same for our own health? If we're willing to help our children, doesn't God want us to do the same for ourselves? Doesn't He want us to seek answers for healing?

What about a career choice? We don't say that if God wants me to be in a different career, it will happen. No, we seek out different opportunities, do our research, and figure out what's a good match for us. If God wants us to do this for our career choices, why wouldn't He want us to seek answers during a health crisis?

You may wonder how much alternative and integrative treatments cost. But I have a question for you: Where did we get the idea that the best care would be fully covered by insurance? I don't know about you, but I want to be free to make my own choices for health and wellness. The costs will vary. I had to be open to learning about the treatment and what the cost would be. After researching integrative treatment and meeting with the doctors, Jan and I decided to proceed with the option that would restore me to health, even if it meant paying for some of it ourselves. In the long run, it was a small price to pay to continue living. To say that you won't spend the money to restore yourself to health without even looking

> *I don't know about you, but I want to be free to make my own choices for health and wellness. The costs will vary.*

at options doesn't make sense to me. If you don't have your health, what good is the money?

Some people have questions about integrative or alternative treatments, but aren't willing to figure out if these treatments would be a good fit for them. They're either coerced into conventional treatment, or they decide to go with the mainstream because it's easier. Again, if you know there are options, I don't know why you wouldn't seek out the best alternatives. Research what you think might be the best treatment for you, follow it through, meet with the doctor, ask questions, find out what it involves, and then determine if it's right for you. How can you know what's best if you don't look at all the options?

I've also been asked what role staying positive and not giving in to fear has played in my recovery. One of the best things you can do is practice gratitude. Gratitude is like skipping. You can't be angry or depressed when you're doing either one. But how can you practice gratitude when you're angry or depressed? One word at a time, either spoken or written. I've been angry and depressed and, quite frankly, I didn't want to be grateful. I was too busy nursing my wounds.

Start by making a conscious decision to be grateful every day. The first day you try this, your gratitude list may be small, but you do have things to be grateful for if you're willing to look for them. If you write a gratitude list every day, your list will grow. We all have ebbs and flows in our lives. Some days you'll be more grateful than others, but if you make it a habit to practice gratitude every day, you'll eventually see a shift in your emotions.

Some things in life seem incredibly heavy. They're almost too big of a burden to carry. But they can be valuable. I can see that I had to overcome this adversity to become the person I am today.

I don't want to sound like I have all the answers. I don't. But I do have questions, and I will keep searching, just as I hope you will.

EXERCISE: CHAPTER 12

We discussed how to look at the six areas of your life. Now let's take a closer look.

- What goals have you set in each area?
- Are they SMART goals?
- Did you rank them in order of importance?
- How badly do you want to accomplish each of these goals?
- What's your motivation in each case?
- Who will you ask to help you on this journey; who will hold you accountable?
- Have you allowed yourself to dream?
- What do you really want to be, do, and have?
- Have you looked six years into the future to see what your life will be like? Have you set goals that will get you there?
- Are they truly your goals, or do they reflect what you think you *should* do or what you think *someone else* wants you to do?

If they're not your goals, they won't excite you or bring passion into your life. If they're big enough to represent your dreams, your goals will be big enough to excite you and maybe even scare you.

Afterword

'</ve wanted to write a book for a long time. In January 2018, while I was still very ill, I signed up for a writing class at Sun City Grand in Arizona. Some days I was too sick to walk or drive the five blocks to class, so Jan would drive me. I was determined to stay active. There were so many things I couldn't do, but I thought, *This is my chance to write a book.* The stories in the beginning of the book are those I wrote in class when I was ill. I thought this book would be about my life growing up and maybe about goal setting and how I got to where I am. I didn't realize that the book would take on a life of its own. Every time I'd write something, I'd hear a voice that said, "go deeper." The deeper I got, the more vulnerable I felt.

Everything in my life had prepared me for this journey. All the times I tried and failed and all the times I tried and succeeded—they all paled in the light of the words, "You have cancer." Yet, I knew everything I'd been through had prepared me for that moment. I had a blind faith in God, and I knew He would lead me to the right treatments and would heal me. I let go and knew I was where I needed to be. This was my new journey, and God had been with me through every other journey before now. I had a new trust. I had nowhere else to go. And I didn't need to go anywhere else because God had the answers.

So much of what I've experienced has been orchestrated by God: the synchronicities that seemed to flow, as well as the major bumps in the road that left me breathless. What a beautiful weaving of tapestry our lives are, if we're willing to change the things we can and accept what we can't. I'm so blessed to have been born in a country where I have the freedom to do the things I've done. Every day of life is a special gift that you can either cherish or take for granted.

> It's so important to be around positive people who will lift you up and not pull you down—people who want to help you. It's just as critical to separate yourself from people with negative energy who deplete you.

I wrote this book to share what I've learned along the way and to tell you that if I can do this, you can, too. If you have a vision, you can make amazing things happen. It's so important to be around positive people who will lift you up and not pull you down—people who want to help you. It's just as critical to separate yourself from people with negative energy who deplete you.

The most important thing I've learned from my journey is to listen to the still, small voice inside. It is God speaking to you. Sometimes you may not want to hear it because the ideas are too big, and you might think, *Who am I to achieve something so grand?*

Other times, the voice will inspire you to help others or to find help for yourself.

Be an advocate for yourself. Believe in yourself and your dreams. What a gift life is! Always remember to enjoy it.

About the Author

After hearing the words, "You have cancer," Mary knew that everything in her life had prepared her for that moment. Her blind faith in God and her focus on the inner voice led her to find integrative treatments for cancer—and they worked!

Mary's vision is to share her story in hopes of helping other people know they, too, have options and can choose what is right for themselves, that they can set their own goals and visualize—and attain—both physical and spiritual healing.

Follow Mary as she takes you through a goal-setting process that will inspire you to dream, visualize, and be your authentic self; to listen to the still, small voice inside and *know* that you have options and can be healed.

Mary lives in Arizona with her husband, Jan, and travels throughout the Midwest during the summer. Mary and Jan have seven children and eleven grandchildren.

You can visit Mary at https://maryrechkemmermeyer.com.

CPSIA information can be obtained
at www.ICGtesting.com
Printed in the USA
BVHW051643090320
574528BV00014B/1559

9 781733 995887